EXPLORING SPACE

FUTURE SPACE MISSIONS

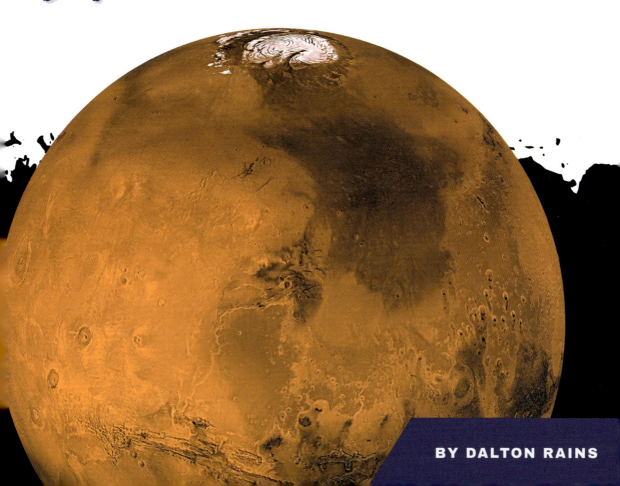

BY DALTON RAINS

WWW.APEXEDITIONS.COM

Copyright © 2024 by Apex Editions, Mendota Heights, MN 55120. All rights reserved. No part of this book may be reproduced or utilized in any form or by any means without written permission from the publisher.

Apex is distributed by North Star Editions:
sales@northstareditions.com | 888-417-0195

Produced for Apex by Red Line Editorial.

Photographs ©: iStockphoto, cover; NASA, 1, 7, 12, 16–17, 18–19, 20–21, 26, 27, 29; Eric Bordelon/NASA, 4–5, 6; Shutterstock Images, 9; Joel Kowsky/NASA, 10–11; Kim Shiflett/NASA, 13; Josh Valcarcel/JSC/NASA, 14–15; ESA/JAXA BepiColombo/Cover Images/ZUMAPRESS/Newscom, 22–23; Bill Ingalls/NASA, 24

Library of Congress Control Number: 2023910082

ISBN
978-1-63738-737-5 (hardcover)
978-1-63738-780-1 (paperback)
978-1-63738-865-5 (ebook pdf)
978-1-63738-823-5 (hosted ebook)

Printed in the United States of America
Mankato, MN
012024

NOTE TO PARENTS AND EDUCATORS

Apex books are designed to build literacy skills in striving readers. Exciting, high-interest content attracts and holds readers' attention. The text is carefully leveled to allow students to achieve success quickly. Additional features, such as bolded glossary words for difficult terms, help build comprehension.

TABLE OF CONTENTS

CHAPTER 1
ARTEMIS III 4

CHAPTER 2
STEPS TO THE MOON 10

CHAPTER 3
MARS MISSIONS 16

CHAPTER 4
OTHER MISSIONS 22

COMPREHENSION QUESTIONS • 28
GLOSSARY • 30
TO LEARN MORE • 31
ABOUT THE AUTHOR • 31
INDEX • 32

CHAPTER 1

ARTEMIS III

In 2017, **NASA** began making plans for a new mission. It aimed to send people back to the Moon. The mission was called Artemis III.

A worker prepares parts for Artemis III in 2021.

FAST FACT
Astronauts landed on the Moon six times between 1969 and 1972.

Apollo 17 took place in 1972. Harrison H. Schmitt was one of the astronauts to land on the Moon.

Astronauts would spend several days on the Moon. They would examine its surface. They'd take **samples** of ice.

◀ In 2022, NASA workers prepared a tank for Artemis III. The tank held the fuel for the launch.

NASA planned for more Moon missions, too. Scientists were working on a **space station**. It would **orbit** the Moon. The station would help astronauts live on the Moon.

SOUTH POLE
In 2022, NASA announced where Artemis III could land. These areas were near the Moon's south pole. This place is covered in shadows. Astronauts planned to use headlamps to see better.

An illustration shows plans for what the Moon's space station would look like.

CHAPTER 2

Steps to the Moon

In 2022, NASA took a step toward Artemis III. It completed a mission called Artemis I. A rocket launched into space. It carried a new **capsule**. No people were inside.

Artemis I's rocket launched on November 16, 2022.

The Artemis I spacecraft took pictures of the Moon.

The capsule flew to the Moon. This spacecraft orbited for six days. Then it returned to Earth. The mission was a success.

SPACE LAUNCH SYSTEM

Artemis I used a new rocket. It is called the Space Launch System. Engines help the spacecraft lift off. Then, they fall off. The spacecraft continues toward space.

The US Navy recovered the Artemis I capsule on December 11, 2022.

The four Artemis II astronauts were Christina Hammock Koch (left), Victor Glover (top), Reid Wiseman (bottom), and Jeremy Hansen (right).

In April 2023, NASA made an announcement. It named four astronauts for Artemis II. They planned to orbit the Moon.

FAST FACT

Three of the Artemis II astronauts were American. One was Canadian.

CHAPTER 3

MARS MISSIONS

Some **rovers** went to Mars. One landed in 2021. It gathered rocks and soil. NASA wanted to study those samples. It planned to bring them back to Earth.

The *Perseverance* rover takes a sample from Mars in December 2022.

In the 2010s, scientists in Europe began planning their own mission. They aimed to study Mars, too. The scientists built a rover. In 2023, they set the launch date for 2028.

In 2018, European scientists announced what part of Mars they wanted to study. The location is called Oxia Planum.

FAST FACT

In 2017, Japanese scientists announced a Mars mission. They wanted to study the planet's two moons.

Scientists want to send people to Mars someday. The Artemis missions might help reach that goal.

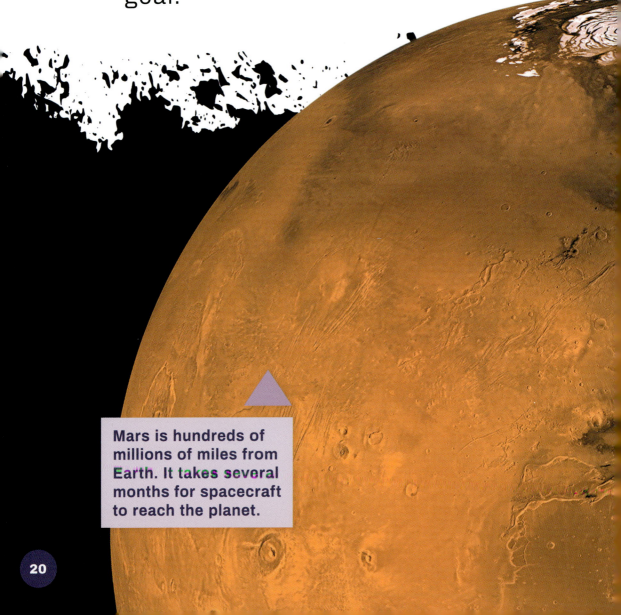

Mars is hundreds of millions of miles from Earth. It takes several months for spacecraft to reach the planet.

LIVING ON MARS

People might be able to live on Mars for long periods of time. NASA made Mars-like environments on Earth. Astronauts lived in them to prepare.

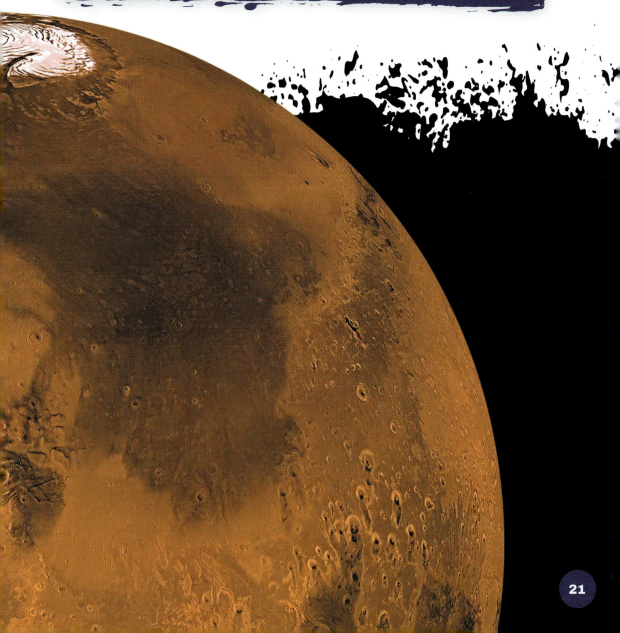

CHAPTER 4

Other Missions

Scientists in Europe launched a **probe** in 2018. The spacecraft began **flybys** of Mercury in 2021. Then it would orbit the planet.

22

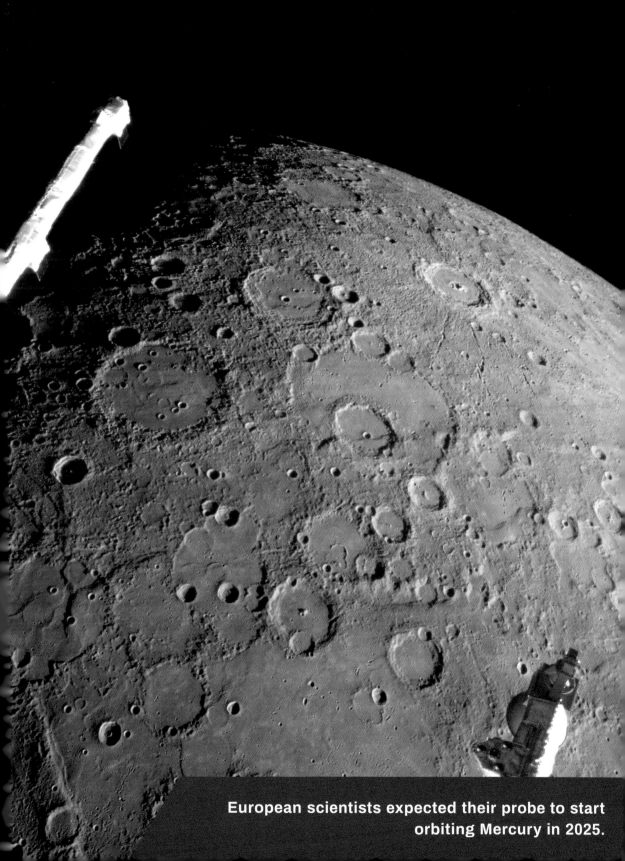

European scientists expected their probe to start orbiting Mercury in 2025.

NASA launched the *Lucy* probe in 2021. This mission focused on asteroids. It was set to last until 2033.

FAST FACT

NASA also worked on sending spacecraft to Venus. It hoped to study water and volcanoes.

Lucy launched in October 2021. It was planned to pass by eight asteroids over 12 years.

Jupiter's moon Ganymede (lower right) is the largest moon in the solar system.

In April 2023, another probe went to space. It was headed for Jupiter. It was expected to arrive in 2031. The probe aimed to study Jupiter's moons.

The Dragonfly mission would explore a moon called Titan.

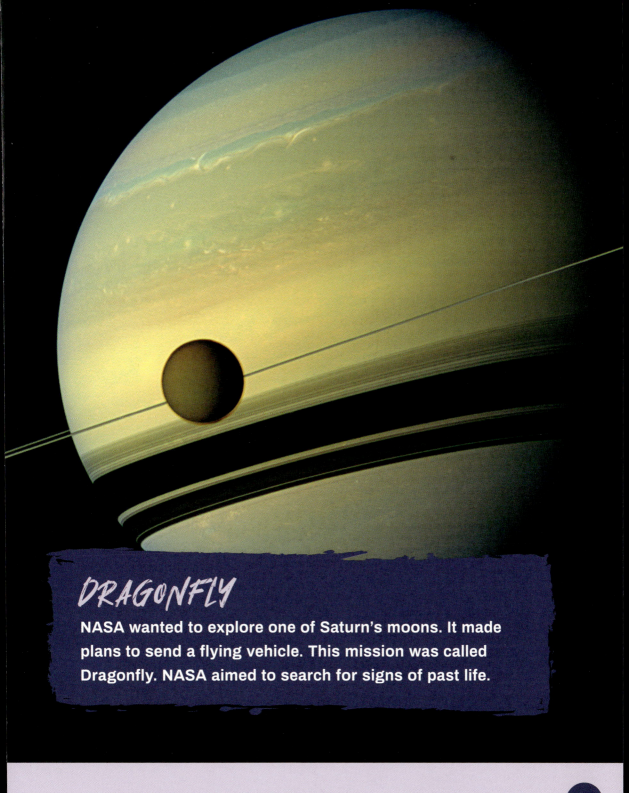

DRAGONFLY

NASA wanted to explore one of Saturn's moons. It made plans to send a flying vehicle. This mission was called Dragonfly. NASA aimed to search for signs of past life.

COMPREHENSION QUESTIONS

Write your answers on a separate piece of paper.

1. Write a few sentences that explain the main ideas of Chapter 2.

2. Which future mission do you find most interesting? Why?

3. When did the *Lucy* probe launch?
    - A. 2017
    - B. 2018
    - C. 2021

4. Why did NASA do two Artemis missions before the mission to land on the Moon?
    - A. to make sure NASA was ready for the Moon landing
    - B. to land on another space object first
    - C. to go back to earlier Moon landings

5. What does **examine** mean in this book?

*They would **examine** its surface. They'd take samples of ice.*

    A. study
    B. launch from
    C. land on

6. What does **environments** mean in this book?

*NASA made Mars-like **environments** on Earth. Astronauts lived in them to prepare.*

    A. the spacecraft used for landing
    B. the features of certain areas
    C. the tools that take samples

Answer key on page 32.

GLOSSARY

capsule
A small spacecraft where astronauts stay.

flybys
When spacecraft fly past objects in space and collect information.

NASA
Short for National Aeronautics and Space Administration. NASA is the United States' space organization.

orbit
To follow a curved path around an object in space.

probe
A type of spacecraft that gathers information.

rovers
Vehicles that explore the ground of other objects in space.

samples
Small amounts of a material that scientists collect and study.

space station
A spacecraft where astronauts can live. It orbits a planet or a moon.

BOOKS

Morey, Allan. *Exploring Space*. Minneapolis: Bellwether Media, 2023.

Murray, Julie. *Rovers*. Minneapolis: Abdo Publishing, 2020.

Stratton, Connor. *Space Exploration*. Mendota Heights, MN: Focus Readers, 2023.

ONLINE RESOURCES

Visit **www.apexeditions.com** to find links and resources related to this title.

ABOUT THE AUTHOR

Dalton Rains is an author and editor from Saint Paul, Minnesota. He loves to learn about new science discoveries.

INDEX

A
Artemis missions, 4, 8, 10, 13, 15, 20
astronauts, 6–8, 15, 21

C
capsule, 10, 12

J
Jupiter, 26

M
Mars, 16, 18–21
Mercury, 22
Moon, 4, 6–8, 12, 15

N
NASA, 4, 8, 10, 15, 16, 21, 25, 27

O
orbiting, 8, 12, 15, 22

P
probe, 22, 25–26

R
rovers, 16, 18

S
samples, 7, 16
Saturn, 27
Space Launch System, 13

V
Venus, 25

ANSWER KEY:
1. Answers will vary; 2. Answers will vary; 3. C; 4. A; 5. A; 6. B